Transmutation
By Ethan Aycock

Spirits

Gallant knight, warrior true.
Evil spirit, renowned and menacing.
Epic battle, time will tell.
That day will come, forever and ever.

Noble steed, fast and majestic.
Trusting bond, old as life.
Emotions bring together
This beast and man.

Swords vs magicn
Battle begun.
Steed suffers crossfire
And is deemed gone.

The loss is heavy
Mental toll billed the knight
Pain internally, and filled with fright.
Can he recover?

He withdrawals from battle,
He suffers his defeat.
He trains to be better
And remembers his noble steed.

He breaks down
Stuck in self destruction,
He is hurt. And
He is doomed.

Time goes on
Evil spirit, renowned and menacing.
Epic battle, time will tell.
That day will come, forever and ever.

This hero is no hero.
This loser is a loser.
This man is weak.
This man is doomed.

He thinks of his pal
Mighty horse indeed.
He thinks of his death
Tragic in all ways.

Through his tears,
Above his pain
He realizes this must end
Spirit shall be cleansed.

So set out on foot;
Walking through the marshes,
Eventually he finds that spirit

And takes his soul.

With his pain, and
With his victory:
He sheds a tear
And feels no fear.

But now he must move on;
His spirit pulled from his body.
He is doomed to protect these lands
Evil spirit, renowned and menacing.

Death

Welcome to the deepest pit of hell.
Get comfy, you'll be here a while.

You see those men over there?
Their souls will be tortured forever.

You see those with no hope?
They love it here, we call them demons.

You see those who can't see?
Pity them, that's their suffering.

You see yourself?
You see your suffering?
You are the devil, you are creating hell.

With Beauty

Here is my confession to you:
I am weak and in pain.
My soul calls for help
I am disabled and immobilized.

I'd ask you for help
To relieve my pain,
But the problem is
I like it.

Which means my pain is pleasure,
And I'm really just fine.
So don't worry about me
Please ignore this lie.

But here is my confession to you:
My pain is my strength
And yours too.
So please, carry on as you do.

Dead Flowers

The following is a tale.

Sar was a prince, a born heir.
His parents died when he was young,
So he rules in his youth

One day he spots a subject
One day he talks to her
One day they fall in love
And some day, they will rule together.

Time goes on; kiss, love, honeymoon.
They enjoy each other's presence.
Both are private, ruling from secrecy.
Both are mysterious, conceiving plans.

They wage wars on nations
And become powerful.
They enjoy good times
And become renowned.

Until one day
Sar finds peace.
He doesn't become wise;
He simply dies.

His fate was tragic; death by wife.
She killed him,
And all their glory.

Times become dark; People scared;
Markets empty; tyranny true.
Times become scary; murder;
Destruction; anger.

She created pain,
And now leads alone,
She now empowers her army.
And is evil.

Her reign never ends;
This is her corner of the world.
All will do as she says;
The Queen of Darkness.

Birth

Thank you Lord,
You have blessed me
You have given me
You have bestowed me.

Thank you Lord,
You are light
You have created abundance
You have called.

Why lord,
Have you cursed me?
Have you taken away?
Have you doomed me?

Why lord?
You are darkness
You have created scarcity
You ignore my cries.

I now understand;
Your methods are interesting.
I see why you work,
I see your goal.

You have made me suffer
So that I can feel.
You have made me weak
So that I can be strong.

As the truth is simple
Be it your word,
You made me crippled
Then you made me the Lord.

Love Triangle

Pain and Misery,
Me and them.
They follow me
I follow them.

We have a love triangle
We do everything together.
They bring me comfort,
And I give them life.

Love and compassion,
My ex-partners.
We had a triangle
But they wouldn't commit.

Pain and Misery,
We are a family.
Pain and Misery,
And me, Triumph.

Outcast

A Lion was banned from his tribe,
Cursed to walk alone.
As his days went on,
He discovered a watering hole.

This place was magic, yet small.
The lion enjoyed his time in peace.
Any animal that came here
Died by the jaws of the beast.

One day, the watering hole dried.
The lion was forced to improvise.
To find new water, or to
Fix this one.

He went on a journey
With starvation and sorrow.
He battled mountains and poverty,
And found a tree in the river.

This tree once stood tall
Now it has fallen.
This tree once drank water
Now blocks the river.

He cleared the barrier
And in doing so set himself free.
He returned to the watering hole
And found the Animal Kingdom.

Instead of killing
He created compassion.
Instead of fleeing
They named him King.

Essence

I am a plant. A piece of grass.
Young, born three days ago.
Since my birth there's only beauty.
I dream of being a tree.

I talk to the others around me,
We get along nicely.
I see cows closely
And wonder if they'll respect me.

One gets close
It's so cute.
One gets close
It chomps 'n' gulps.

I feel so much pain
These teeth tear me apart.
Forced down his throat
Into an ocean of acid.

I feel myself dissolve
I see my friends suffering too.
I become one with them and acid
Then we are turned to poo.

Humiliated in front of others,
Those not swallowed.
We come out as shit
And will be tomorrow.

Cows and humans walk on us,
Welcome pain and unease.
We question why and if it ends;
Then it rains and rains for days.

Weeks go by, no end in sight
But as we seep into the ground,
I feel magic all around
And that magic scares away fright.

Weeks go by, I see the light.
I have fertilized a seed; now one.
I grow strong and tall, mighty too.
I have sprouted:
Please call me Spruce.

Time

In the beginning
There was darkness.

And in the ending
There will be light.

Centrifugal

Think abstractly,
I am abstract.
Think gravity,
I am a force.

As the world spins
I am pushed away.
As the world turns
I fight to the center.

Everyday, closer I become.
To give up. I would be flung.
I want to throw everyone on earth
And gravity pulls against me.

This is not easy,
But I don't want to bore you.
So wait for when I am center
And I will become.

Fighting

A seed was planted.
That seed was young.
It's will is to grow,
So grow it will.

Days went on
Months flew by
Trees got taller
Grass got greener.

This seed, it fought through doubt
Fought through drought
Fought through flooding
Fought through pain
Fought through sorrow
Fought through violence
Fought through gore
Fought through setbacks
And fought through the soil.

But after everything
That seed did sprout and grow.
Because despite all that suffering
That seed was you.

Circles

The days run together
They all look the same.
Time falls like a feather
Each day has the same pain.

Life goes one,
Great days and bad.
But the little details
They seem to repeat.

Big events happen of course.
Plans change and people grow.
Each day doesn't get a memory,
Just those of special, and of crow.

So Laugh,
Live
Love
Lust
Lie
Linger
And laugh
All emotions come back again
We go up and we go down.

Take things in stride,
Nothing is permanent.
Love yourself,
And be born to be alive.

Shed

Here, there is only darkness,
The only company; demons.
Here, you must survive,
The only company; inner hellion.

Cruel, dark, twisted.
Cold, lonely, shallow.
Empty, broken, starving.
This is not where you want to be.

Monsters seep from the abyss.
Your own breath visible.
Light does not touch here,
Neither does happiness.

Evil lurks; defeat present.
You'll wish this was death.
Ages go on; torture is endured.
Pain.

After an eternity
Your cocoon sheds.
Light breaks and
You are now a butterfly.

Self

Thunder cracks and rain falls
The man rides through.
The moon is new; midnight.
What horrors await?

Down the cliffside
Up the mountain.
Across the plains and
Through the rivers.
Keep marching.
The men need us.

The hero arrives;
There is a battle.
This is a great war,
The hero draws sword.

He fights; and they fight back.
Who will prevail?
Metal clings; men yell.
Who will perish? Who will survive?

Many die; the man lives.
He fought with all might.
He beat his demons;
Victor of inner war.
And now, King he is crowned.

Man Made Misery

Living lavishly and loving life.
Entertainment and exotic eating.
Partying powerfully;
Playing potently.
Life is good.

Life is almost too good,
No struggles or sympathies
No resistance or restriction
No problems or poverty.

What do I do?
Everything is easy; lame and lux.
I get so bored
Because I always get what I want.

Then it hits me!
That's the problem:
There is no problem.

So, here I go.
I'll create my own problems;
Man made misery.
Then rise above I will.

Extraction Zone

Hot hours under shining sun.
Heaps of sandstone scraped.
Moving mountains and discovering
Dark secrets.

In the middle of a harsh desert,
Under boiling heat with little water.
Small shelter with desert storms,
Sand that stings; rattlesnakes.

My team and I dig.
We turn over large stones,
Move piles of sand.
We find nothing that matters.

We've been here for months,
Always an empty hand.
Everything is so hot and hard,
I might just give up.

But then,
We find it:
Inner-strength.
And all its beauty.

Kingdom Call

I am a prince. My father a king.
I have everything I could want:
Women, money, food, anything.
I am on top of the world.

Everyday I go out, I enjoy myself.
Everyday I sleep in, I need rest.
Everyday I do what I want,
Everyday I wake, I rule the world.

Father dies unexpectedly: battle.
Mother dies expectedly: plague.
I now have kingly responsibilities.
I am terrified of what's coming.
I have no one to help me;
No one to trust.

Things get dark; my parents died.
Things get heavy; I lead a nation.
I am not sure what to do.
The pressure is too much.

As days go on, nights get long.
I watch myself become my father.
A mighty king; destined I am.

The Plunge

I come across a cavern; a ravine,
A crack in the ground runing deep.
I dismount and take a peek.

It's dark. I can't see the bottom.
Lightning shoots down
Into the abyss.
The way is lit; for a moment I see.

The crack is deep:
Monsters and demons reside.
I see their ugly faces;
Spiders and mummies tell lies.

A wail of cries and zombies,
Deep water and death,
A group of men waiting for
Speech.

Single women awaiting approach,
Poltergeist; sin; speed; heights.
I see it all, vast before me.

Then it occurs!
This crack is not real, I made it up.
And it shows my fears.
With that, I take the plunge.
With that, head first I dive.

Fire

Furious flames of fucking fury
A ball of fire like the sun.
Anger seeps in all directions
Like the blood barreling in veins.

Little things set people off
Pet peeves piss emotions.
Anointed annoyances
Allow agony.

Yeling ugly curses;
Demeaning in our heads.
Hitting things
And wishing they were dead.

The fire increases in size
Ignites all that it touches.
Bigger and bigger
Hotter and hotter.

But soon resources dry out
And the flames down.
Now it's all over; the fire gone.
And the world is left cold.

New

Strong winds and dark skies
Loud lightning with
Theatrical thunder.
Downpour; a flood may be among.

Water levels rise; cities sink.
Farms flooded and houses,
Everyone flees the scene
Except those that die.

Days pass and it rains more,
Nights go on while water fills all.
When will this nightmare end?
Abundance creating madness.

Ships destroyed; villages in ruin;
Trees broken; families separated;
Life struggles; all in pain;
This may be the end.

But rain stops; the sun comes out.
Once things dry, they being anew.
Communities with exotic crops;
The world reborn.

V=IR

I zap down to the earth in great
strides and create pockets of
intense heat that explode and ring
true my name across the minds of
those that can hear. I have been
around for a very long time, and
there are fundamental laws that
govern the way that I am able to
behave. I strike wherever I please,
but the feierosty of which is
determined by another, outside
component: Resistance, or the
flow of energy against me. The
more of that there is, the better.
Infact, if there were no resistance,
I wouldn't exist, and neither would
you.

On and On and on

My lord, you must pardon the interruption, the men at the gate have called for help, they are being attacked by a despicable and ravaging beast from the nearby forest that has 8 eyes showing respect to the 8 Gods, 6 arms that slither across the ground and pulls the center belly toward its target, and a jaw that detaches so that the creature may swallow it's victims whole while they scream as the enter first the mouth of this satanspawn, then into the throat where they fall unconscious due to the levels of carbon produced by stomach acid, that will dissolve the poor soul then use the acid produced by the body dissolved at a later time by regurgitating through its eyes, to fire on other creators, predators, prey, or currently the group of men stationed at the gate, located about 10,000 feet south of our location, attached to two 70 foot walls, which stretch on and on and on, encompassing the entire kingdom and all its subjects, approximately 500,000 civilians, all of which live their lives day to day in the same stuck routine and spent all their time on lame activities such as wand sharpening, where the entire industry has been reformed to create a standard that makes the elves happy by qualifications of the product, but pays little attention to the working standards that dwarfs are stuck slave to and endangering their well-being by placing them in a location near radioactive waste produced by a source of magic, a very powerful source of magic, used to power all wands in the kingdom and stretches back to the beginning of time, where some say that this magic was placed here before the creation of the universe, by God himself, then he used this magic to create the universe and all the living souls in it, which happen to be the elves at the time, and they then used it to create the dwarfs for the purpose of beings slaves, where they are stuck in their same old routines, going on and on and on forever, stuck, like mud, unable to get out, unable to die, made immortal by the magic of the elves, so they don't have to maintain the population and will have slaves until end of time, or until, which happened recently, the dwarfs realized their immortality and fought ruthlessly through a large war, killing many elves until they reached the source of magic, and they used it to create a new world, one where there will be no elves, where there are dwarfs and only dwarfs, and of course the slave race of humans that they created, but then the humans overpowered and did the same thing but created a slave empire of orcs, who also did the same things but with goblins, who also did the same thing but with elves, and this cycle went on and on and on, like the lives of those who live in the civil empire, or even those of the slave empire, because that's all they do, go about their same old routines and patterns and habits, and make no attempt to change.

But, we can change
You me him or her
We are powerful.

If you deem change,
Then deemed.

You just have to deem it so
And that is scary.

But there is good news,
And you've heard it before
But this time, please hear it;
You are powerful.

Cage

A castle is located in the desert
There are four walls and a throne.
A king sits on that throne
And that king has a pet bird.

That bird is small
And mimics words to all;
He sits in his cage all day
At night he dreams of play.

One day, the maid left latch open
And the bird escaped.
He flew through the castle
Then out the window.

Once outside, he flew for freedom.
Once outside, he was confronted:
A wall of flame,
Keeping the castle safe.

Land and contemplate;
Almost returning to cage.
Fear crept in the mind
And immobilized the brain.

Until he summoned all courage
And took the leap of faith.
Entering the flames was painful
And burned off all feathers.

But survive did he
And emerge he did.
Not just as a bird,
As eternal phoenix.

Sea of Scorching

I have been walking for days.
I have no destination.
I travel for fun
And lay out in the sun.

Over mountains and rocks
You've heard it all before.
I am traveling far away
And always wanting more.

I walk walk and walk
Until I can walk no longer.
I eat eat and eat
Until I can eat no longer.

I come upon the desert:
Hot and hellish.
I know its reputation:
Devilish and deadly.
But I know no fear:
Neither here nor there.

After what seems like ages,
Many moments or months,
I run out of water, and emerges
My fear.

I fear my death, but death isn't
scary.
I fear my thirst, but scarsity isn't
scary.
I fear my pain, but hurt isn't scary.
I fear the inevitable, but
Bravery I have.

Walking on, marching forward.
Everlasting desert:
Heat and sorrow.
Will this be my end? Or
Will it be our beginning?

After ages of aimlessly aching
And angishing,
I decide no more.
I lay down in defeat,
And decide no more.

Upon my death wish
Another was granted.
I look in surprise
And find an oasis.

Filled with water, trees, animals.
I run fourth to play, splash, drink.
I enjoy myself, then
Decide it's time to nap.

I dream of an empire
One ruled by me,
I dream of prosperity
In the middle of a sea.

When I wake, I look around.
All other animals, being profound.
I am in the sea, one of danger
And of luminosity.

I decide it's here, a place of
dreams.
I decide right now, a time of
growth.
The desert is harsh, this oasis
lush,
This is the island in my sea.

So the empire, built I deem.
And beginning now, all are
Welcome under one condition.
They must cross the
Sea of Scorching.

Advert

A ghost reaches for you
But you advert.

A demon charges you
But you advert.

A monster whispers to you
But you advert.

A ghoul listens to you
But you advert.

Monsters demons ghouls ghosts,
Many things want to get you
But you must advert.

Trust the process
Time will tell
Advert.

Until you see the light
And the hand that reaches
Grab hold and follow
And soon you'll emerge.

That hand pulls you
And brings you true.
You now exit the womb.

Create

I wave a wand and make a wish,
Think a thought, send a setting.
Hope an ending and
Begin a beginning.

Everything around; created you.
Around everything; you created.
The birds, the bees,
The girls, the trees,
You made all and all made you.

You created this life
You made you
You created your loved ones
You made us.

Take a walk
Think a thought
You'll soon see
It's all for you to be.

So enjoy, you
Go fourth, create!
The worlds a blank slate;
And you're holding the brush.

Natural Disasters

In the earth's mighty spin
Things get pushed around.
Tectonic plates slide
Here comes an earthquake.

The ground shakes; on an island
A volcano is pushed to erupt.
A spew of lava comes out
And fire rains down.

Desecration in every direction,
Damage all around.
Fire in trees and
Flames on buildings.

Thankfully,
The same earthquake;
Makes a tsunami.
And it barrels fourth.

Massive waves; crashing forces,
The water and the lava meet.
A dance of hot then cold,
And now new land is great.

Blizzard

Snow falls and covers the earth;
Everything cold and frigid.
Silence engulfs; magic enchants;
Snow falls and covers the earth.

No one goes outside.
No one drives.
Everyone stays inside.
Everyone sleeps.
Trees collect snowflakes;
Branches ice.

The sun is below the earth,
The moon is new; planet dark.
Yet everywhere you look - a glow.
Tonight, earth is covered in snow.

It keeps going; mounds taller,
Ice and snow everywhere.
Right now is dangerous
To be outside.

So everyone is inside,
Hot chocolate and pajamas.
Everyone is cozy
With gifts and movies.

The Wall

"We can't go there now" said Jim, while stuffing a handful of popcorn into his mouth. "The wall has been formed, it's huge and massive and everything in between." No response. Jim is actually talking to himself. He's trying to decide if he should go to this mystery location. Just one problem, other than his indecisiveness, the wall! The wall blocks everything and everyone. I'm not sure if I've ever heard of anyone getting past the wall, and I'm the concept of time, so I'm old. Jim sits there for a while, then decides to go, but by the time he reaches his conclusion the wall is gone. Jim, in his surprising disappointment, is sad. He realizes that the wall was the best part. The only reason he even wanted to go was to confront the wall, but now it's gone. "Hmmm…" Jim thinks. "Ah hah!" He turns on his shower, freezing cold. He gets naked and thinks "I don't want to do this." And with that, the wall appears.

Dear Reader

Love is a tricky thing, dear reader.
...It creeps up
on you...

It'll eat you.
Dissolve you.
Digest you.

It'll spit you back up; reject you;
become hate.

What do you love?
sweet; Or Sour?
Honey; Vinegar?
Roses; or thorns?

I'll share what I love,
Please don't laugh.
I love a person, a special one,
With beauty and amaze.

The entire universe within your
Eyes.
I love them, this person; you, dear
reader.

Hell

Anger. Hate. Lust. Vile.
We reside in the dark
Amongst demons and monsters.
No fear is here, not from us.

Evil everywhere.
Death too.
It's all disturbing
Concerning too.

Shadows and souls
Ghosts and ghouls
Fire and fury
A person and their obituary.

Cold. So cold.
Alone. So alone.
This place: Horrid
Run away, don't return.

Among the dark
Along the mourn,
This place is special
It's where angels are born.

Fuel

Strong is true
Tall and wide.
Up and far; in fiery few.

Force beware
Your devilish touch; evil soul
Don't come at me
Because I'll eat you.

You see young lad,
You can not grow,
Get strong or true
Without some resistance; reverse
pull.

Resistance will make you grow
Hard times powerful
Sad times loving
Easy times happy
And scary times fuel.

Don't be afraid,
It'll make you, you.

Deep

Deep in the crust of the earth
There lies me, a piece of coal.

Deep under pressure
There lies magma, waiting to cool.

Deep in the ground
Waiting for me.

Deep deep deep
Cold coal and dark.

I am pushed into magma
Thanks to the pressure.

With this heat and this tension
Only one thing is bound to
happen.

That would be my transmutation
From coal, to diamond.

He

This plant stands tall,
He is mighty and brave
Conquering and loving.

He enjoys a peaceful life;
A slab of heaven.
This plant is powerful
And lives in prosperity.

You might ask;
How can I do so too?
Be warned; learning how might
Deter you.

All of life this plant has struggles
But none of them compare to birth.
Born in a place of darkness
And from a seed split in half.

The first battle of all,
The induction to life
Was the hardest for he
And deemed him mighty.

Prowess

A young man is being brought up
He experiences pain and neglect.
He fights on everyday,
Determined to be
Great and powerful.

A young man is bullied everyday,
Torture from peers and
Refuse from leaders.
Determined to be
Great and powerful.

A man enters boot camp
A true warrior.
His comrades tease and poke,
His generals are too hard.
Determined to be
Great and powerful

A man enters battle
He kills many
His allies turn on him
And leave him behind.

Alone,
No one but him.
He fights to survive,
Determined to be
Great and powerful.

Alone,
Determined to be
Great and powerful,
He learns the ways of magic
And conducts a ritual.

A demon, ugly and horrible
Steals life from those
Who wronged him.
Determined to be
Great and powerful.

Feeding on souls;
Growing in strength.
Until one day; become the devil
Great and powerful.

Myth

Hear me, I am Zeus
God of thunder and sky
Fear me, I am God of all
And king of Gods.

I do what I please
And the humans sing about me.
I am who I am
Father of mankind.

Great, powerful, lustful,
My brothers below me
Epic, demanding, strong,
Humans are to serve me.

Until that fateful day,
I don't know what happened
All was good
Now all is dull.

I was a legend
And respectfully so.
Now the songs change
And I am a forgotten myth...

Field

A beautiful sunflower sprouts,
Grows from the ground and
Reaches its head up,
Joining its brothers and sisters
In the Field of Sun.

A field full of magic and beauty
Existing in the world as a haven.
Many times has this place healed
Those who have fallen.

Day after day, sunflower after
Sunflower.
The field is everlasting, and
Growing larger.
But this awesome miracle, it won't
Last forever.

During a drought, lightning strikes.
Igniting a forest,
The world ablaze.
Soon, a ring of ash surrounds the
Field.

Water is cut off
No rain in months.
The fire burned all the trees
And now the field thirsts.

Slowly and painfully,
The magic seeps.
It leaves the field as
Everything dies.

Soon the field is no more
And only ash lies in its place
Animals venture in, to
Find their fate.

This once amazing place
Now a forsaken land.
The Field of Sun
Now Field of Sorrow.

Cancer

All things are temporary
Nothing is forever.
This includes pain and suffering
And also pleasure.

A dean to a college,
Living life with potential
Sudden migraines and headaches
Leads to discover a brain tumor.

Doctor says not long,
Tumor rapidly growing.
You may have 6 months,
Or less and counting.

Once the tumor gets so big
Two things happen:
First the man forgets his childhood
Second he becomes brilliant.

During his final months
He makes discoveries;
He teaches the world new science
And engraves a new philosophy.

He writes books and dictionaries.
He received a Nobel prize.
The college becomes renowned.
And then, he dies.

Full Bloom

The town council all in meeting
Five men and no women.
They talk about the fate of town
And how the growth has stunted.

One fellow, mad man if you will,
Suggested an idea, crazy you'll
find.

Why don't we take the town, with
All its current glory and
Infrastructure, science and
Architecture, military and defense,
Women and children.

Why don't we take it, and return to
Ashes. Our growth is stunted,
What more can we do?

Let us hit the reset button.
Start something new,
And from the remains
We'll grow to full bloom.

Memento Mori

Here is a simple idea
Please follow with imagination.
We will create an imagine
Then have it as you will.

Death; gross and upsetting.
Think of a skull, a pile of ashes.
Place a flower, its pedals full;
It sprouts from the remains
And grows through the skull.

Dance

Step
    By
        Step

We

    Will
        Love.

Story

Simple beginning
Tragic middle
Humble end.

I'm stuck in thought.

Then I learn.

Coming of

A birthing of a man
Creation acting into;
World realization and exaltation.
Actions actualized and concepts
Conceptualized.

Your simple idea, bringith true
Upon divine right, do what's you.
Be the creation of beings and act
upon thy universe as you please,
do as immortals do, I gift unto
thee.

Take your world into your hands.
Hand your world to its taker.
Become into gravity
And radiate away later.

Blast your senses into oblivion and
wear good fashion, go all that way
and go that way.

Now I hand you the reins, and give
yours.
Be who you are; you who that be.
Welcome your way as a wondrous
waxing.

Leap

What you are about to experience
Will be very difficult.
Now enter a sacred ritual,
Associated with our tribe for
Hundreds of years.

Today is your day to compete.
Bring yourself to life.
Harness the magic in the air;
Wield it, and go fourth godly.

You will begin with feeling pain.
Deformation: welcome new limbs
Sprout from your torso.

Then you will lose thy breath
And any attempt to breath is
Punishable by death.

After so you will faint, then
Waking in a world unfamiliar
With strange beasts.

...

Now that you have woke, you may
Experience your powers as a
Newborn frog.

Internal

A world away, light years beyond.
Something exists and persists,
Fighting on and on.

Deep into space, a
Concentration of matter.
A force like gravity and
Power electricity.

It lives and thrives;
Indulged and exasperant.
It finds a welcome in
Darkness.

Evil and all bad,
Once there and full;
Now is gone thanks to this
Mysterious power; you.

This world, it's your brain.
This space, it's your mind.
The power inside you are;
Pushing out evil from the dark.

Down River

A river flows down the
mountainside, crashing into
everything it hits. Lunging forward
and captivating all that exist.
Within that river is a small fish,
swimming upriver, against all flow
of the universe; embracing what is
thrown; seeing skyscrapers,
ranches, cattle, hospitals,
churches, trees, rocks, asteroids,
moons, planets, atoms, and
quarks. Many lifetimes go on
before the fish can rest, she will
face challenges fit for heroes,
dilemmas fit for philosophers,
problems fit for engineers, fire's
firefighters; criminals cops; tests
students; lesson plans teachers;
moons planets; and quarks fit for
atoms. Once finished, she will
rest. But during that rest she is
doomed to feel the pain of
needles, axes, screwdrivers,
wrenches, acid, bleach, water,
piss, scratches, eyes, toes, womb,
eggs. Now she may die peacefully,
and her children will be born and
receive the once-in-a-lifetime
pleasure of swimming down river.

Moon Pool

Mirror of water, upon approach I
see my reflection, and I look
straight into the pinnacle of my
being, being blasted backward
internally as my gaze comes upon
myself, and recognize the deer,
elk and moose that exist in me,
the world infinitely small within.
Once my sight sets I realize the
reflection being broadcast now,
and it echoes across the night sky.
The universe has become aware
of itself.

Burrow

A burrow of dead trees exists at
the forest center. Ugly images of
death and decay protrude at every
sight. A small patch of sand takes
the place of a small hole, where
water used to reign.

The trees no longer stand tall, they
lean over and sweep the ground
with their brittle branches. They
snap and break, throwing out
sound like thunder and leaving a
dramatic show for any that find
themselves lucky to watch.

As change goes, things here will
not remain the same. Lightning
strikes, igniting and spreading,
consuming and controlling. Great
heat takes over, burning all that
lay here, creating piles of ash.

At the center of the forest there is
a meadow of ash, and with time
that graveyard will become lush.

Great

The white shark, swimming along
in his domain. Eating smaller fish,
and not gaining in size. Teenage
shark has much to learn.

Weather above; the surface gets
harsh. A storm rattles the waves,
and creates new currents, which
further cause the waters to spiral
into an uncontrollable maelstrom,
surely to sink anything.

The white shark, swimming along
is caught in the disaster, pulled to
the ocean floor and pinned under
its own weight and lack of upward
force.

Days of trap and starvation, and
the shark comes close to death.
Summoning all strength and frees
himself, swimming away and
finding prey, so that much needed
energy will be replaced.

This white shark, once born of
spoilage, now has faced a right of
passage deemed by the earth and
universe. This white shark, now
great and glorious.

Harmony

Before the world was walking
And the wonders waking,
There was nothing but darkness
And the life that lived inside.

Creatures of the dark,
Disturbing and dank.
Creatures of the night,
Must soon bring light.

So, the bacteria came together
Created a new form of life: water.
So, the bacteria came together
Created a new form of life: air.

Air and water mingled, and soon
Earth was born.
Still darkness, until bacteria was
Able to come together in the
Manifestation of man.

Man came upon the earth and saw
The future. Still dark and cold,
Something must be done.

So man grew a brain, and that
Brain was powered by electricity.
By wielding the power of lightning,
Man created fire, and gave light.

Now with magic, bacteria was able
To create all that it needed, from
Earth to fire, life tingled and
Existed in harmony.

Down

A simple man lived in his castle,
and loved his wife. That love
created a child, an heir to the
throne.

The prince lived lavishly, and
received anything he wanted. The
prince more godly than kingly.

Using his god given powers, he
attained pleasure so immaculate
that it became pain.

Pain from pleasure, no more
pleasure, only pain.

The pain became intense, and
increased with every indulgence
that the god believed would solve
his pain - until his parents died
and he became king.

Still ruling as a god, he found a
simple pleasure where there
should be pain - the death of his
parents.

So he killed, and killed again. This
became his legacy.

So reign on as lord, and take what
thy please. A new generation is
upon the world, and the lord rules
as the devil.

Center

You go on about your day,
Creating and destroying.
You go on about your night,
Sleeping and studying,
Building a life.

But you do one thing wrong
And unfortunately you don't see it.
And because of that problem, you
Are stuck in self-destruction.

I wish I could tell you of your
Problem, but you don't listen.
And unfortunately, you're part of
the problem.

You could try to learn of it, but
Doing so wouldn't fix anything,
In fact you'd make it worse.

You don't just have a problem, you
Are the problem. You're my
Problem and my friends too.

You see here, problem, your
Problem is that you are the
Problem, and by being the
Problem you create problems for
Everyone around you.

But problems help us grow,
Mistakes learn, and set-backs
Move forward. Embrace your
Problem to become a truer you.

And by being a problem for others,
Receiving hate and love, you do a
Miraculous thing.

You cause others to grow, you're
The water for dirt and sunlight for
Plants. You are the medium of
Growth for the whole world.

So, I'd tell you about your
Problem, but you don't listen, I
Won't waste my breath.

But here's one thing I say to the
World, and not you. Embrace your
Demons and cast out the light,
Because by doing so you come
Back better.

Thank you, problem, for being my
Center. And thank you, for growing
The whole world.

Hero

You is hero.
Hero is strong.
Strong is growth.
Growth comes from weak.
Weak is life.
Life is you.
You is hero
And hero is you.

Where Does It Come From?

The world can be dark and lonely,
When the lantern is off.
Without heat and power outside;
The internal a beacon of light.

You tell me;
Is that a good thing or bad?

Here is Your Quest;

Be sent from ashes and rise anew.
Be sent from God and create.
Be a demon of light; go forth to
Extinguish the warmth of all.

Here is your quest;

I send you to perform a task.
That task is to help and heal
The children of me and you.
Show them the power of darkness.

Here is your quest;

Be born and struggle,
Live in pain and anguish.
Be created and tortured
Then die in peace and power.

Find my children, you their father.
Be mean and frightful, evil, deadly.
Break their souls and spirits
So that they'll transform lovely.

Here is your quest;

Create a world of love, luxury;
Take this word of peace, positivity;
Ignite it, drown it, destroy it.
Be a phoenix in the night
Cause rebirth; then you can come
Back and be God again.

Diplomacy

Call me emperor, and let us discuss these simple diplomatic terms of peace over in my gazebo. Call me emperor and tell me of your plans to avoid war. I fear you have no ability to avoid the disgusting aspect of leading a nation, especially when the only reason your nation is capable of surviving is by selling your goods at a discounted price, exclusively to me, and if you decide that you would rather not, then you shall meet my army of men and robots, prepared to take you down.

Call me student, I wish to learn from you as I grow a nation of greatness and rule the world from a golden throne. Call me student, I wish for you to teach me the ways of creating prosperity for myself and others.

Call me emperor, watch as I do now and you will be met with destruction. Call me emperor and go fourth to the one you call farmer, he will teach you of trying to reap what you did not sow, and that your nation will be met with famine.

Call me student, teach me the ways of growth and I shall sell my nation's goods to you.

Call me emperor and you shall sell me your goods for free and live under my colors, as a colony. Call me emperor, I will teach you, but you must fear me.

Call me student; now call me enemy. I will not rule under you; I am prepared to fight you. I

understand now, and your death will be my reap.

Call me teacher, you have learned my lesson. You see the light, but now you must fight. Your nation will be met with armies, of me and allies. Your nation will not thrive.

Call me enemy, as I learn the ways of war.
Call me enemy, as I learn of poverty.
Watch me, as I build a nation built on the backs of difficulty, as my people will experience death and destruction. We will be broken and hurt, but we will come back, as the student becomes the master, and my empire will be built on the back of yours, my father.

Crops

I dream of being a farmer. I have
bought some land, tilled it,
fertilized the soil, and acquired
one seed. From this seed I shall
grow a city, and that city will be full
of luxury. An entire field of crops
shall grow from this seed, and
from that field another and
another. I march out to my center,
say a little prayer, and place the
seed into the ground. Then comes
rain, fertilizer, more rain and
compost. No sprout. I talk nicely
to it and pray for it; no sprout. I
summon energy of growth and
give unto thee; no sprout. I grow
angry. I flood the land, cover it
from sun. I destroy the till and
curse the seed. I shout, scream
and cry. Why is there no growth? It
has everything it needs. I neglect
the plant, I stop watering it, no
more fertilizer, and no more help.
I don't know what happened, but
overnight the seed sprouted and
grew, now ready for harvest; like
magic. I reap and plant two, but I
begin with neglect instead. Now,
overnight, four plants have
miraculously sprouted. So I
neglect more, and the organisms
take control of their fate, and
repopulate the whole field in a
matter of a week. I treat them
harshly, and push them to be
better. I love them, but it's tough.
Now my field is lush, my city
growing, and people asking me:
How do you achieve growth?

Tandem Harmony

From the demands of the clouds,
The rain beats down for months.
The world floods, no ground above
This is no longer earth, land of dirt.

From this suffering:
Trees grow from below.
Stretching tall and reaching for air;
Coming from water.

At first weak but then sound,
More and more come from below.
Earth had land, now only water,
Yet life has still made its way.

This planet; transformed.
The jungle from the ocean.
New life teams the trees and lives
On, in tandem harmony.

Spring

The more energy you fight me with
The harder I bounce back.

Us

The apes; their good source gone.
A young ape; wants to help.
Bananas; at the top of a tall tree.
Climb; dangerous.

Young ape thinks of the risks;
Possibly a fall,
Maybe death.

But the benefits will be survival,
Ape continuation.

The ape climbs; furthest ever.
Others watch; tallest timber.
He almost falls; adrenaline!

Soon he gets the bananas
And returns to his people.
Young man earned their name;
The Great Apes.

Poem; Short; Guide.

Suffering; growth; thrivance.
Pain; pleasure; life.
Up; down; circle.
Leader; outcast; transmute.

Fire; pressure; diamond.
Food; shelter; chrysalis.
Strength; weakness;
perseverance.
Love; hate; fuel.

Pain; misery; triumph.
Orgasm; pinnacle; death.
Boredom; thought; creation.
Past; future; infinite.

You; me; God.
Us; them; all.
Me; myself; powerful.
You; yourself; strong.
Everyone; everything; relate.

That and More

Here's the path; quick and hard:
If you want to achieve all you can;
Follow this trail with perseverance:

Rocks in front of you, hot.
Go barefoot, then to the
Walk of spikes.

After that you will face
Obsidian shards and a
Pool of lava.
Walk through it all
Burn your soles.

Once you cross the ocean of acid,
The valley of lightning,
The mountain of explosions,
And the casm of void,

You can enter the pool of healing
And receive everything back.
That and more.

As Below; So Above.

Place of darkness;
Creepy crawlies and
Damned creatures.

This is your home and
You've always been here.

One day; everything usual
You are entombed in a rope
Wrapped round and roped.

Thorns inject into you
And begin to drink your blood.

Soon you die, by the vines
And your life force sucked out,
Into the branches above.

You are part of the tree now,
You stand tall and in light.

Grim

This is morbid; and I'm sorry
You have to learn this truth.
But I created you and all,
For my personal benefit.

You see, I am not really a person,
Animal or plant.
I'm a force of nature, I take souls.

I created all, I was there at birth.
Throughout your life I fed you,
Gave you power and thought.
Now you are strong, able, ripe.

Now it's time to end; call me
Death.
I sowed you,
Now be ready for reap.

Fix

Have you ever thought about how
the day begins and ends in
darkness? Or how the jungle
comes alive at night? That a
butterfly is formed in a cocoon, or
life egg?

Have you ever wondered where
you are? Standing on a mountain
or the bottom of a river? Have you
considered the possibility that
maybe what you see isn't real?

Chances are it isn't, and when you
understand that your mind will
break. But broken things can be
fixed, and usually will come back
better.

So break your mind; lose it.
And when you fix it,
I will call you my Lord.

Gleam

The brightest star
Can only be found
In the darkest skies.

Thankful

Thankful for this day
Thankful for tonight
Thankful for this life
And thanks for the light.

But also;
Thank you for the night; demons;
Monsters and fright.
Thank you for sorrow, tears, sulk
And wallow.
Thank you hard times, struggle,
Heartbreak and trouble.

Thank you for the lessons,
Thanks for teaching me,
Now that I've struggled I can
Live free.

Smelt

I am lost in a dark space.
I can not move and am suffocated.
I live down here always,
I wish I could leave.

Someone found me, but no ally.
I am stuck with sharp weapons,
Bagged and gagged; taken.
Away we go, I wish I could leave.

I arrive at another dark place,
Only the red light from the fire.
My bounds still unbroken,
And now tossed in the fire.

Everything burns and melts away,
I can feel the power of purification.
Everything hurts
And now becomes liquid.

As I molten,
A hammer strikes.
Over and over
Until I break.

Then more heat, another hammer.
I meet an anvil; water.
Taken through a painful process.
Emerge; I went from ore to sword.

Pattern

In order to stand, you must come
from below.

In order to walk, you must have
been still.

In order to talk, you must have
been quiet.

In order to love, you must have
been hated.

Do you see the pattern?

Unrepulsive

Guiding me down this path;
The trail of broken souls.
She beckons my name;
I won't heed the call.

Syren screams from parted lips
Pitchful paradox; do that, not this.
Aching affirmations; wanting you.
A menacing minotaur,
Maddening most men

You do have one good quality;
You create stronger people.
The pressure makes diamonds;
You are the resistance that flows.

So live on; call to all.
Suck them in, steal their soul.
Create demons; destroy angels.
Wage war on women and
Worry men with woes.

But one thing is certain:
You win battles; not wars.

Cold

The freezing cold
Pushed away.
The freezing cold
Unwanted.

Unloved with no heat;
No one wants you.
No touch, no feel,
That's the life of the cold.

Living in the shadows
Awake at night.
Only in the north,
And far south.

Hidden in remote regions
Nowhere to be found.
The cold stays away;
Knowing itself dangerous.

But there's one other place that
Cold is found.
In the homes of great men,
And it's welcome anytime.

Poetic Justice

Iron is material.
It's Sturdy. Heavy. Simple.
Iron is powerful
Trustful, resilient, understanding.

Fire is immaterial
It's Fierce. Fine. Fast.
Fire is powerful
Emotion, love, language.

        Fire and Iron
They do a dance
          fine and sturdy.

        Stone and flame...
            ...Tango
Understanding and love...

These two beings; they
Exist in us all.
Live simple and fiercely
Have resilient emotion.

Dance their tune;
And prosper.

Questions

What is peace and quiet?
What is loud and proud?
Are they the same
Or are they not?

What is the problem
With unidentification?
Why can't you or I
Remain anonymous?

What does the sky look like at
night?
The sun up close?
The moon far away?
Or myself in the future?

Where do we go when we die?
Where does love come from?
Is any of this real?
Can I kiss you tonight?

I have no answers.
Only questions to be.
So tell me
How are you?

Lesson

Entertain while bored
Have fun when dying.
Sulk when happy
And land while flying.

Eat while hungry
And cook when not.
Play tag with frenemies
And cry when not.

But most importantly:
Live while alive.

Tectonic Plates

The ground began flat, and the
entire world went on for one
elevation. But with the movement
of time and the forward of earth,
the ground was twisted and turned
to shape. While everything went
crack and boom, the ground rose
up. While things began to sink and
swim, the ground solidified. With
great disfiguration the floor
becomes old and unfamiliar, yet
new and nostalgic. Upon this flat
earth you live, the ground will now
introduce an inspiring message;
call it mountain.

State Change

Ice is cold.
Apply some heat and now
It's water.

Gate

If death is dead
And life is living
Evil is bad
And good is holy,

Then prosperity is holy
And suffering bad.
However, one is the gate
For the other.

Length

Stuck high in a tower
With a bald head,
She was determined to make her
escape.

So years went on
Famine and filth,
Time passed by
Her hair grew well.

After a long time of struggle and
Pain
Her hair was now long enough to
Rapel
She she cut it and built a
Rope
And lowered herself
Out.

Once on the ground
Via time of hair and growth,
She had the world in her palm
Free to go.

Change

When it burns
Grass grows greener.

When it floods
Crops grow taller.

When it dries
Everything becomes conserving.

And when we feast
We understand the pain.

Your Battles

Look at how far you've come.
Look at your victories,
Look where you succumbed.
Look at you now.

Unity

1
Come 2.
Come 4.
Come infinity.

All is one.
But in order to do that
One must become all,
By painful division.

Tell Me

Lies hold you back
Truth propels you forward.
But deciding which is which
That will be the struggle.

It's almost impossible
To distinguish.
Really it comes to your belief
Which is the most powerful?

So you tell me
What do you believe?
Are you held back
Or moving forward?

Rain

Think of the climb
A drop of water must make
If if ever wants to experience
The free fall of rain.

Down Then Up

As things divide smaller and
Smaller, and as the world gets
Ever larger and larger,
Think of your place and if it grows
Or shrinks, and think of you; who
Makes that choice.

Growing is great, prosperity
Will come; but shrinking is great,
Growing will come.
One can't get bigger
If it doesn't first get smaller.

All for One

Leafs burn in the sunlight, and
Melt under water.

The seed is one; it sprouts.
The roots become a trunk,
Which becomes many branches,
Which become many leaves.

All the many leaves are in pain
Melting and burning.
But they endure this pain
To feed the seed.

Adapt

An overload of good things;
Great food and wonderful wine.
A spoilage of spirit and pleasures
Has led to a doomed fate.

Sensory organs deprived,
Filled with the miracle of life.
Dopamine and serotonin
Have reached new heights.

The more I adjust
To the way things are.
The closer I come
To an ultimate and epic
Self destruction of soul and love.

As pleasure leads to pain,
I shall hold head in sorrow.
I indulge in my pities,
As pain leads to pleasure.

Spring

Standing here on this hillside
Watching out upon the world.
I see many species of animals
As well as plentiful brethren.

But here comes that wretched foe,
The one I welcome open.
Here comes wicked warmonger,
Whose presence shall enlighten.

The beast has massive wings,
Capable of hovering flight.
The creature has a needle,
protruding from its nose.

I know that all will be ok, that
All will grow. This beast is a
Hummingbird; come to take my
pollen.

Goddess

The ants enjoy great perks:
Grand civilization, food and drink.
Colony bread abundant,
And no one feels pain.

This is only possible thanks to the
Queen; glued to the throne and
slave for the people,
Day round and all night.

Perched high, surrounded.
Always laboring always.
Endures pain, excruciating.
Her children running, free.

First Come

First winter then summer,
Bring night then day.
Enjoy fall then spring,
Sorrow then gay.

Welcome suffering then love,
Have pain then peace.
See ugly then beauty,
Be cold then have fleece.

Hear cries then song,
Feel lonely then friendship.
Indulge in pity
Then realize empathy.

Leave, Have, Take

Leave luxury to lame leprechauns
And let lonely light a lingering fire
That leaches out and lives.

Have homage for hell and hate,
Heal to helios and heat,
Help the hellion have his honor.

Take time and tension:
Transform into theme.
True life teaming with tea:
Taken unto temperance.
Transmute things tearfully:
Team up with tired,
Thinking things thoughtfully.

Made in the USA
Las Vegas, NV
19 November 2021

34767234R10056